Introduction

How do the different provisions of a 401(k) plan affect the participation rates of employees? As traditional pensions continue their long decline and various changes to Social Security are contemplated, this question is becoming increasingly crucial to those concerned about the sufficiency of retirement savings among US workers. In 2003, 39.9 percent[1] of U.S. private industry workers had access[2] to a 401(k) plan in which employees were required to voluntarily make contributions in order to participate, with employers matching some of those contributions made. Yet, only 67.9 percent of those with access to these plans participated; among lower-paid workers, the take-up rate[3] was even lower (59.6 percent). These facts have fed the concern that many workers may be saving too little for retirement and strengthen the imperative for plan provisions that promote participation effectively.

Although the literature has produced a variety of different estimates of how different 401(k) plan provisions affect participation, a particular picture of the broad contours of these effects has been consistently portrayed in a number of papers by Choi, Laibson, and Madrian. Primarily exploiting an extensive administrative database[4] linking employer-, plan- and employee-specific information, these authors have argued convincingly that a significant fraction of workers, disproportionately having relatively low incomes, act passively with regard to their 401(k)-related saving decisions.

---

[1] Author's calculations using the National Compensation Survey (NCS) microdata collected from newly-initiated NCS sample members in 2003.
[2] Access to a benefit plan is defined in the National Compensation Survey according to the presence of a plan in the job/establishment pair; some workers are defined as having access even if they do not meet the applicable eligibility requirements.
[3] The take-up rate is defined in the National Compensation Survey as number of participants divided by number of workers with access (see footnote 1 above).
[4] Choi, Laibson and Madrian make repeated use of administrative data collected by Hewitt Associates, a large human resources consulting company, from some of its clients.

Consistent with this behavior, Choi, Laibson, and Madrian find that a) the rate at which employers match employee contributions has, at most, a moderate effect on participation; and b) the institution of automatic enrollment has effects that are quite large. For those primarily interested in encouraging saving among the relatively less well-paid, this has led to the conclusion that automatic enrollment provisions are the best approach. Accordingly, in recent years legislative changes have aimed at encouraging automatic enrollment provisions[5], and the prevalence of such provisions has grown rapidly. Beshears, Choi, Laibson, and Madrian (2007) have additionally argued that the presence of automatic enrollment diminishes the need for employers to provide generous matches; if this logic is widely adopted, declines in match rate levels might be expected in the future.[6]

But since the evidence assembled by Choi, *et al* is not based on a representative sample of workers, its generalizability to the U.S. population remains in question. Indeed, other studies that have used different data samples have produced a wide variety of different results. Some of these studies have been consistent with the findings of Choi, *et al*: Kusko, Poterba and Wilcox (1998), using administrative data from one employer, Munnell, Sunden and Taylor (2001/2002), using 1998 Survey of Consumer Finances data; and Mitchell, Utkus and Yang (2005), using administrative data from Vanguard, all find that employer match rates have relatively small effects on employee participation and contribution rates, if they have any effect at all. But other studies have contradicted

---

[5] For example, in 2006 the Pension Protection Act established a new avenue for employers to obtain "safe harbor" status, which allows an employer to automatically satisfy the plan's non-discrimination requirements. The requirements for reaching the safe harbor originally specified in 1996 included a potential employer match of 4 percent of pay, but the new law allows the safe harbor to be reached with a potential match of 3.5 percent of pay if enrollment is automatic.
[6] See, for example, Powell (2008).

this finding. Using administrative data from Watson Wyatt, Clark and Schieber (1998) find that employees receiving a 50-75 percent match are 28 percentage points more likely to participate than employees receiving a 25 percent match. Using data from the Health and Retirement Survey, Cunningham and Englehardt (2002) estimate that (unconditional) employee contributions were increased by about 19 percent by the employer matches observed in their sample. None of these studies examined the effects of automatic enrollment provisions, but the variety of estimates of matching effects suggests that further testing of the automatic enrollment measures of the Choi, *et al* studies is also needed.

In addition, different studies have employed different methods, causing different biases to be admitted in the estimates, or estimating parameters that are altogether different in concept. For instance, Basset, Fleming and Rodrigues (1998) use 1993 CPS data to estimate a small impact of employer matches on employee participation rates. But Even and MacPherson (2005) use the same data, with a different methodology, to estimate that the presence of an employer match increases participation by 32.8 percentage points. Englehardt and Kumar (2007) find modest effects of matching on saving, despite the sizable effects on plan contributions estimated by Cunningham and Englehardt (2002) using the same data. Papke (1995) produced two sets of measures from 1985-1986 IRS Form 5500 data; one set shows that employer matches play a large role in employee participation decisions, while the other indicates little or no effect.

In this paper, a large, nationally representative dataset from 2002-2003 is exploited to provide measures of the effects of 401(k) plan provisions on the participation rates of employees. The dataset contains sufficient details to estimate the effects of several dimensions of employer matches, providing some leverage for disentangling the direct effects of the provisions on participation from effects that operate through sorting. It also allows estimation of the effects of automatic enrollment provisions, so that comparisons of the magnitudes of these effects are feasible, as well as investigation of some other plan provisions that are sometimes found to be important. Finally, the unique structure of the dataset and linkages between the dataset and a larger survey of defined contribution costs allow the employment of instrumental variables to obtain estimates of the true treatment effect of employer matches on employee participation.

The results of the study reinforce those of Choi, *et al* in some important ways: automatic enrollment provisions have substantial effects on plan participation, especially among relatively less well-paid workers. And among such workers, the generosity of employer-provided match rates does not seem to affect participation at all. But the results also show that match rates *are* an important motivator for some workers – those with intermediate levels of pay. Among this group, the effect on participation of increasing the match rate may be even greater than the effect of instituting automatic enrollment. This suggests that matching contributions still have an important role to play in stimulating retirement saving.

Data

The data come from the National Compensation Survey (NCS), a large, nationally representative survey conducted by the U.S. Bureau of Labor Statistics. Data from the NCS is used to calculate the Employment Cost Index, which estimates the growth in compensation costs, including those arising from employer-provided benefits, for a fixed bundle of workers. The NCS is collected with a rotating panel design, with a new panel initiated approximately once per year. When a panel is initiated, brochures for employers' benefit plans are collected along with the employer cost and benefit participation information. The details of these plan brochures are coded into the NCS database, and the incidence of various detailed plan provisions are reported in official bulletins. In this study, we use NCS microdata from the respondents initiated in 2002 and 2003, focusing on the detailed provisions data collected from 401(k) plan brochures and the contemporaneous participation data collected from the corresponding establishments.

The NCS microdata are collected at the job level: within each sampled establishment, a small number of narrowly defined jobs are selected.[7] The resulting wage, benefit costs, and participation data consist of averages among the employees at the establishment having that job description. This sample design allows participation behavior to be associated with job attributes such as average wage rates in the job. However, it does not allow consideration of differences between workers' wage rates within the job, nor to account directly for some other pertinent worker attributes such as age.

The focus of this study is on one variant of 401(k) plans: the savings and thrift. Such plans entail voluntary (tax deductible) contributions by the employee that are matched to some extent by the employer. This is easily the most prevalent form of 401(k) plan, making up more than 80 percent of 401(k) plans in which the employer

---

[7] Depending on the size of the establishment, between 1 and 8 jobs are sampled.

made some contributions in 2002-2003.[8] Not included in the study are plans to which employers make no contributions, which are also fairly prevalent.[9] Among savings and thrift plans, there is substantial variation in the way that the employer match is determined. The majority of plans have a flat match profile – one percentage is applied to each employee's contributions, up to a specified percentage of the employee's salary. But a significant minority of plans applies a variable match rate, where employees receive one match rate to a first amount of their contributions and another (usually lower) rate on additional contributions, up to some limit. A smaller minority has different match profiles for different employees within a job, depending on the employees' tenure. Still others have matches that vary from year to year, depending on employer profits or simply the employer's discretion. This last group of plans is dropped from the sample; the others are included.

Table 1 provides some summary statistics about the plans in the sample.[10] 82 percent of the sample is made up of 401(k) plans with flat match rate profiles, while 13 percent have match rates that change over the range of contributions made by employees, and the remainder has match profiles that depend on the employee's tenure. The average match rate on the first dollar contributed by employees is 75.37 percent, while the last dollar matched receives an average match of 68.64 percent.[11] Plans in the sample

---

[8] Author's calculations using the National Compensation Survey (NCS) microdata collected from newly-initiated NCS sample members in 2002 and 2003.

[9] In 2005, an estimated 16 percent of private industry workers had access to cash deferred arrangements with no employer contributions. These are not considered to be retirement benefit plans by the BLS. (BLS Summary 05-01). For more details about these "zero-match" plans, see section 9.5 of Holmer, Janney and Cohen (2008).

[10] For a more detailed presentation of the match provisions of these data in which weights have been used to allow estimates of prevalence among all US private industry employers, see Dworak-Fisher (2007).

[11] In order to calculate measures among the plans whose match profiles vary by tenure, we imputed the tenure distribution of each corresponding record based on the available information and detailed occupational averages, then averaged the match provisions across these imputed distributions.

provided matches on employee contributions up to 5.16 of the corresponding salary, on average. Combining these provisions, we can determine the maximum potential matching contribution made by the employer under each plan. The average of the "potential percentage match" in our sample is 3.57 percent of salary. Converting this figure in dollars by multiplying it by the hourly wage times 2,000, the "potential dollar match" averages $1,657 in our sample.

Some other characteristics of the sample are also visible from Table 1. These include several additional provisions of the 401(k) plans: a very high percentage of the sample (85%) indicates that employees have some choice over how their own contributions are invested; a slightly smaller fraction (75%) indicates employee control over the employer's contributions; 70 percent allow employees to draw loans from their 401(k) accounts. A small percentage of the plans in the sample (6 percent) are governed by the automatic enrollment provisions advocated by Choi, *et al*. There is also a good deal of information about the compensation received by employees on these jobs: 40 percent of the jobs indicate that they also provide a defined benefit plan, while only 21 percent provide an additional defined contribution plan.[12] The average observation has a wage of $22.66 per hour, a health benefit costing the employer $2.21 per hour worked, and a defined benefit cost of $0.52 per hour worked. Total compensation for this sample averages $33.10 per hour worked. The data also contain detailed (6-digit) occupation and industry identifiers, as well as the location and employment of the establishments and

---

[12] A very small fraction of sample members have more than one savings and thrift plan. In such cases, we focus only on the plan that had the highest participation rate.

whether workers in the job are unionized. The sample consists of 2,708 jobs in 587 establishments[13], with 67 percent of jobs observed in 2003 and the rest observed in 2002.

The dependent variable in the analysis is the participation rate for each job, defined as the fraction of workers in the job that participate in the plan. This variable can generally be considered a take-up rate, as almost all employees in a job with access to the plan are eligible. Yet, some plans have eligibility requirements based on months of service. The average participation rate in the sample is .72.

There is a significant amount of variation in the sample in both the match provisions and in the participation rates observed. Figure 1 shows the frequency distributions of the first dollar match rate, the potential percentage match, and the observed participation rate. One important feature of these distributions is that they exhibit spikes at round-numbered values, such 50 and 100 percent match rates and integer values of the potential percentage match. Most important, note that the participation rate distribution has significant mass points at the extremes of the distribution: 29 percent of the observations have a participation rate of 1, and 6 percent have a rate of 0.

Model of Participation in Employer-Provided 401(k) Plans

Determination of Participation

Consider the participation decisions of workers in a given establishment offering a plan with given provisions. In particular, focus on the matching provisions of the plans, letting the other plan provisions be secondary considerations. To start, think of the matching provisions at employer k as being defined by one generosity parameter, M_k,

---

[13] This sample reflects all NCS sample members initiated in 2002 or 2003 for which valid data on match rates and participation were collected, with 1 establishment dropped due to outlying benefit cost values.

that is positively associated with both the percentage match rates applied to employee contributions and to the total potential employer contribution to each plan. Employer k also has other relevant characteristics, including observed characteristics such as other provisions of its 401(k) plan, denoted as E_k, and those that are not observed, such as its "culture" as regards retirement saving, denoted as c_k. Worker i in job j at employer k determines whether or not to participate in the plan according to M_k, E_k, c_k, and his own attributes – both observed attributes such as his income level, denoted as X_i, and unobserved attributes such as his innate attitude toward retirement saving, denoted as a_i. Letting P^*_{ijk} be desired participation rate of worker i in job j, we have:

$$E\left[P^*_{ijk}\right] = \beta_0 + \beta_1 \cdot a_i + \beta_2 \cdot X_i + \beta_3 \cdot c_k + \beta_4 \cdot E_k + \beta_5 \cdot M_k \qquad (1.1)$$

However, this desired participation is not observed. A convincing series of studies has demonstrated that many workers are passive about putting their participation decisions into action: they are quite likely to remain at whatever participation (and contribution) level has been established by their past decisions and (especially) the plan default. To incorporate this behavior into the model, let actual participation P_{ijk} be updated (to P^*_{ijk}) in time period t with probability δ. The Expected Value of P_{ijk} at time t is thus:

$$E\left[P_{ijkt}\right] = P_{ijkt-1} + \delta \cdot \left(P^*_{ijk} - P_{ijkt-1}\right) \qquad (1.2)$$

Letting n_{ijk} be the tenure of worker i in job j at establishment k and P^D_k be the default participation decision at establishment k, the participation probability observed at any point in time is:

Among establishments appearing in the sample in both years, only 2003 data were used.

$$E\left[P_{ijk}\right] = \begin{array}{l} \xi_{ijk}\beta_0 + \xi_{ijk}\beta_1 \cdot a_i + \xi_{ikj}\beta_2 \cdot X_i + \xi_{ikj}\beta_3 \cdot c_k + \xi_{ijk}\beta_4 \cdot E_k + \\ \xi_{ikj}\beta_5 \cdot M_k + \delta^{n_{ijk}} \cdot P^D_k \end{array} \quad (1.3)$$

where $\xi_{ijk} = (1 - \delta^{n_{ijk}})$.

A simplification that allows us to aggregate this expression up to the establishment level in a tractable way is to assume that the n_{ijk} is independent of the other explanatory variables. Let $\bar{\xi}$ and $\bar{\delta}$ be the mean values of ξ_{ijk} and $\delta^{n_{ijk}}$, respectively, across all workers. Letting $\bar{a}_{jk}$ and $\bar{X}_{jk}$ be the mean values of a_i and X_i, respectively, within job j at establishment k, the expected participation rate among workers in establishment k is:

$$E\left[P_{jk}\right] = \begin{array}{l} \bar{\xi}\beta_0 + \bar{\xi}\beta_1 \cdot \bar{a}_{jk} + \bar{\xi}\beta_2 \cdot \bar{X}_{jk} + \bar{\xi}\beta_3 \cdot c_k + \bar{\xi}\beta_4 \cdot E_k + \\ \bar{\xi}\beta_5 \cdot M_k + \bar{\delta} \cdot P^D_k \end{array}. \quad (1.4)$$

Determination of Matching Provisions

There are competing explanations for why employers offer matching provisions in the 401(k) plans they sponsor. One explanation is that employees demand the match as a preferred form of compensation. As Brady (2006) describes, matching contributions by the employer increase the amount of employees' compensation that is allowed to be tax-deferred. Employees might also value the employer match as a means of motivation for their retirement savings, or consider a high match as a signal of employer generosity in general. This explanation is consistent with the results of the Employee Benefit Retirement Institute's 2002 Small Employer Retirement Survey, in which the majority of respondents cited employee recruitment and retention, employee attitude and performance, or employee demand as the most important reason for offering a plan. Another explanation for the provision of M_k is portrayed by Ippolito (2002), who provides evidence that Defined Contribution plans disproportionately attract "savers" and disproportionately result in quits among "spenders." Since "savers" are more productive on the job than "spenders," employers who offer Defined Contribution plans may enjoy a more productive workforce.

Either of these stories may be sensibly extended to the determination of 401(k) match rates, providing a rationale for the diversity of plans observed in the country. If employees of some establishments effectively demand matching contributions while others do not, then it is likely that employees at different establishments might effectively demand higher match rates than employees at other establishments. And if some employers find the differential effects on workforce recruitment and retention great enough to offer a defined contribution plan while others do not, then it is likely that different employers will find different matching incentives to be optimal. In either scenario, employers determine M_k to maintain a workforce with particular tastes for saving in a 401(k) plan, with higher values of M_k corresponding to higher average preferences for saving among workers at employer k.

A natural corollary is that employers must also account for the actions of their labor market competitors in determining M_k. Let O_k represent the generosity of other employers in the same labor market as employer k. A higher value of O_k will cause employers trying to meet the demands of their workers to offer a more generous match, all else equal. Alternatively, an employer attempting to differentially attract high savers must offer a more generous match the greater the value of O_k. Given this consideration, the determination of match generosity can be represented as:

$$M_k = \gamma_0 + \gamma_1 \cdot D_k(\bar{a}_k, \bar{X}_k, O_k) + \gamma_2 \cdot c_k + \gamma_3 \cdot E_k + \gamma_e. \qquad (2.1)$$

where D_k indicates the effective "demand" for matching contributions by the workers at establishment k, as well as the productivity incentive given to employer k to provide generous a match arising from the "differential" preference of savers for such matches. The arguments of D_k include the weighted averages $\bar{a}_k = \sum(s_{mk} \cdot \vec{a}_{mk})$ and $\bar{X}_k = \sum(s_{mk} \cdot \bar{X}_{mk})$, where s_{jk} is the employment share of job j at employer k and m is an argument of summation. The employer characteristics variables c_k and E_k are also included in equation (2.1) to account for miscellaneous heterogeneity in employers' tastes for providing generous 401(k) matches.

Assuming $D_k(\bar{a}_k, \bar{X}_k, O_k) = \psi_0 + \psi_1 \cdot \bar{a}_k + \psi_2 \cdot \bar{X}_k + \psi_3 \cdot O_k + \psi_e$, we have:

$$M_k = \begin{array}{l}(\gamma_0 + \gamma_1 \cdot \psi_0) + \gamma_1 \cdot \psi_1 \cdot \bar{a}_k + \gamma_1 \cdot \psi_2 \cdot \bar{X}_k + \gamma_1 \cdot \psi_3 \cdot O_k \\ + \gamma_2 \cdot c_k + \gamma_3 \cdot E_k + (\gamma_e + \gamma_1 \cdot \psi_e)\end{array}. \qquad (2.2)$$

It is instructive to split $\bar{X}_k$ into two terms, $s_{jk} \cdot \bar{X}_{jk}$ and $\bar{X}_{\sim jk} = \sum_{m \neq j}(s_{mk} \cdot \bar{X}_{mk})$, representing job j's share and the share of all other establishment k jobs in the average characteristics of workers at establishment k, respectively. With this change, the match determination equation becomes:

$$M_k = \begin{array}{l}(\gamma_0 + \gamma_1 \cdot \psi_0) + \gamma_1 \cdot \psi_1 \cdot \bar{a}_k + \gamma_1 \cdot \psi_2 \cdot s_{jk} \cdot \bar{X}_{jk} + \gamma_1 \cdot \psi_2 \cdot \bar{X}_{\sim jk} \\ + \gamma_1 \cdot \psi_3 \cdot O_k + \gamma_2 \cdot c_k + \gamma_3 \cdot E_k + (\gamma_e + \gamma_1 \cdot \psi_e)\end{array}, \qquad (2.3)$$

or, condensing the terms,

$$M_k = \begin{matrix} \eta_0 + \eta_1 \cdot \bar{a}_k + \eta_2 \cdot s_{jk} \cdot \bar{X}_{jk} + \eta_3 \cdot \bar{X}_{\sim jk} + \eta_4 \cdot O_k \\ + \eta_5 \cdot c_k + \eta_6 \cdot E_k + \eta_e \end{matrix}. \qquad (2.4)$$

Application of the Model to an Empirical Setting

Equations (1.3) and (2.4) together describe a model that can be used to relate the values of M_k and P_{jk} observed in the labor market. One application of this model is to shed light on the results of the cross-sectional analyses conducted in much of the literature on the effects of matching on participation. In such analyses, the participation rate of a group of workers (say, P_{jk}) is regressed upon the match rate they face at their current employers (M_k), with controls for observed worker and employer traits (X_{jk} and E_k). This type of analysis has been carried out using data aggregated up to the employer level (Papke, 1995; Clark and Schieber, 2002; Mitchell, Utkus and Yang, 2005) and data observed at the individual level (Munnell, Sunden and Taylor, 2000; Basset, Fleming and Rodrigues, 1998), with varying functional forms (OLS, Probit, etc.).

Consider the following establishment-level OLS equation:

$$P_k = \alpha_0 + \alpha_1 \cdot \bar{X}_k + \alpha_2 \cdot E_k + \alpha_3 \cdot M_k + \varepsilon_k, \qquad (3.1)$$

where the error term ε_k includes all of the unobservable factors such as $\bar{a}_k$ and c_k. As much of the literature has noted, the parameter of interest from this equation (α_3) does not yield an unbiased measure of the pure treatment effect of the match rate on workers, due to the presence of unobservables in the error term and their correlation with M_k. The true value of α_3 can be expressed in terms of the model's parameters as:

$$\alpha_3 = \bar{\xi} \cdot \left(\beta_5 + \beta_1 \cdot \frac{R^2_1}{\eta_1} + \beta_3 \cdot \frac{R^2_5}{\eta_5} \right), \tag{4}$$

where R^2_k indicates the partial R-squared associated with the k-th term in equation 2.4. For instance, the $\beta_1 \cdot \frac{R^2_1}{\eta_1}$ term in equation (4) captures the effect of high unobserved savings preferences being associated with increased match rate through job search – sometimes referred to as the "sorting effect." The $\beta_3 \cdot \frac{R^2_5}{\eta_5}$ term adjusts similarly for unobserved (and correlated) employer characteristics – for example, the effect of employers' enthusiasm for encouraging saving, which might manifest itself as both high match rates and a high amount of encouragement to save being given to employees.

Note that the definition of the pure treatment effect is ambiguous – it depends on what affected outcome is of interest. To capture the effects of M_k on the *intentions* of workers to participate, an uncontaminated measure of β_5 is needed. But the effect of M_k on the average worker's *behavior* is more accurately captured by $\bar{\xi} \cdot \beta_5$. Alternatively, to evaluate broad-based policy ideas such as those that would provide government matches on individuals' IRA contributions, we would be interested in a version of $\bar{\xi} \cdot \beta_5$ in which $\bar{\xi}$ were calculated by extending the adjustment of savings over a longer horizon.

In addition, employers themselves may not be interested in the pure treatment effect *per se*; they are more likely interested in a measure that also includes the sorting effect. For instance, if an employer were considering raising its match rate to achieve a higher participation rate (perhaps in order to meet non-discrimination requirements), it would be interested in both the direct effects of the match increase on current workers and those that would raise the participation rate through worker turnover. For such employers, the object of interest is $\bar{\xi} \cdot \left(\beta_5 + \beta_1 \cdot \dfrac{R^2_1}{\eta_1} \right)$. If the magnitude of $\beta_3 \cdot \dfrac{R^2_5}{\eta_5}$ is negligible – e.g., if unmeasured employer characteristics that also affect participation directly underlie little of the variation in employer matches – then this might not differ much from the simple cross-sectional estimate described in equation (3.1).

Estimating the effects of match rates without the influence of the sorting effects requires an alternative methodology. A common approach in the literature is to analyze changes in participation behavior brought on by changes in the match rate within employers. This approach is used in an analysis of many employers by Papke (1995) and in case studies of individual employers by Kusko, Poterba and Wilcox (1998) and Beshears, Choi, Laibson and Madrian (2007). Such a differencing approach may net out the effects of unobserved worker and employer attributes if these attributes, a_k and c_k, remain constant for the sample studied. There are some concerns about this approach, though. First, if the change in behavior is observed over a short period of time, then the measured effect will be especially attenuated by workers' inertia. For example, an analysis of participation changes over one unit of time will produces a measure of $(1-\delta)\beta_5$ rather than $\bar{\xi}\beta_5$. Studies that have used this approach have tended to use such short-term changes, perhaps in part because of the need to hold the observed sample constant.[14] Second, the underlying assumption that the unobserved employer characteristics, c_k, remain constant in these studies may be questioned. For instance, it seems likely that changes in the provisions would be accompanied by changes in other aspects of the employer's communications with its employees about the plan. This concern is magnified by the inherently diminished scope of variation in match rates. Finally, studies that focus only on a small subset of employers may not be representative of the larger population; if they are focused on particular employers who change their match rates for idiosyncratic reasons, the results might also be idiosyncratic. For example, if changes in match rates are precipitated by unsatisfactorily low participation rates, then these analyses will draw on observations from a particularly unresponsive population.

The model directs us to several other avenues of inquiry that might help us isolate the direct effects of the match provisions on 401(k) participation from the sorting effects. The most immediate remedy to the omitted variable problem is to find additional controls for the variables omitted by other studies. We explore this approach in the empirical analysis to follow by distinguishing different components of the compensation paid to workers in a job.

A second approach is to differentiate between the forms of M_k appearing in equations (1.3) and (2.4). In equation (1.3), the M_k term reflects the match rate's effect as a marginal incentive to save at least one dollar. The specific form of the plan's match provisions that best captures this is the first-dollar match rate. In contrast, the "potential

---

[14] An exception is contained in Choi, Laibson, Madrian and Metrick (2001). Using a hazard model to analyze employees of a firm that introduced a relatively modest match to its 401(k) plan, they project that participation rates rise by 40 percent within the first 2 years. Presumably, this effect would continue to

percentage match" described above may *not* matter in equation (1.3), except to the extent that it reflects a higher match rate. For example, Choi, Laibson, Madrian and Metrick (2001) find that changing the match threshold without changing the match rate elicits no change in employees' participation. In equation (2.4), however, M_k is meant to capture the overall generosity of the plan, which may be best encapsulated by the total potential percentage match described above.

To formalize this notion, let F_k represent the first-dollar match rate and T_k the total potential percentage match at employer k. Then the determination of the match parameter by employers is represented by:

$$T_k = \begin{aligned} &\eta_0 + \eta_1 \cdot \bar{a}_k + \eta_3 \cdot s_{jk} \cdot \overline{X}_{jk} + \eta_4 \cdot \overline{X}_{\sim jk} + \eta_5 \cdot O_k \\ &+ \eta_6 \cdot c_k + \eta_7 \cdot E_k + \eta_e \end{aligned}. \qquad (2.5)$$

Further, let T_k and F_k be related as

$$F_k = \lambda_0 + \lambda_1 \cdot T_k + \phi_k. \qquad (5)$$

In equation (5), ϕ_k captures random variation in the first-dollar match rate *not* associated with the selection and retention of workers with higher savings propensities. Substituting this expression for M_k in equation (1.4), we obtain

$$E\left[P_{jk}\right] = \begin{aligned} &(\bar{\xi}\beta_0 + \bar{\xi}\beta_5\lambda_0) + \bar{\xi}\beta_1 \cdot \bar{a}_{jk} + \bar{\xi}\beta_2 \cdot \overline{X}_{jk} + \xi\beta_3 \cdot c_k \\ &+ \bar{\xi}\beta_4 \cdot E_k + \bar{\xi}\beta_5\lambda_1 \cdot T_k + \bar{\xi}\beta_5 \cdot \phi_k + \bar{\delta} \cdot P^D_k \end{aligned}. \qquad (1.5)$$

Equation (1.5) can be estimated using an OLS equation such as

$$P_k = \alpha_0 + \alpha_1 \cdot \overline{X}_k + \alpha_2 \cdot E_k + \alpha_3 \cdot T_k + \alpha_4 \cdot F_k + \varepsilon_k. \qquad (3.2)$$

---

grow if the projection were carried out for even longer, but the authors note that such projections are speculative.

If there is no residual correlation between ϕ_k and ε_k, then $\hat{\alpha}_4$ is an unbiased estimator of $\overline{\xi}^L \beta_5$.

A third approach to measuring the effect of the employer match on employee participation that follows from the model is to use the measurable factors appearing in equation (2.4) – O_k and $\overline{X}_{\sim jk}$ – to instrument for M_k. We explore this approach as well in the empirical analysis to follow.

Empirical Analysis

Standard Measures

An appropriate way to measure the cross-sectional effects described in equation (3.1) is to implement the Bernoulli Quasi-Maximum Likelihood Estimator (BQMLE) developed by Papke and Wooldridge (1996). The BQMLE deals appropriately with fractional dependent variables having masses in the distribution at 0 and 1. Assume that the expected value of P_{jk} is captured by the standard normal cumulative density function conditional on the specified explanatory variables (Z_{jk}):

$$E(P_{jk} | x_{jk}) = \Phi(Z_{jk}\beta). \tag{6}$$

The BQMLE is computed by maximizing

$$\ell_{jk}(b) = P_{jk} \log[\Phi(Z_{jk}b)] + (1 - P_{jk})\log[1 - \Phi(Z_{jk}b)]. \tag{7}$$

Table 2 gives the estimated average partial effects (APE's) of this cross-sectional analysis, using the log of the first dollar match rate as the key explanatory variable. In the first column, the match variable is entered with only controls for year of observation and eligibility requirements of at least 1 year of service.[15] The results indicate that a doubling of the first dollar match rate is associated with a 5.90 percentage point increase in workers' participation.[16] As illustrated in equation (4), these effects include the impact of sorting arising from workers' choices of employers, as well as any correlations between unobserved employer characteristics affecting participation and the match rate.

In the second column, controls have been added for observable employer characteristics E_k. These include (1-digit) industry, region (9 Census divisions), establishment size, and other provisions of the 401(k) plan. If these controls are comprehensive enough, then we can interpret the resulting estimate of the match rate's APE as the treatment effect plus the sorting effect – the total effect that employers might be interested in. The estimate shows that a doubling of the first-dollar match rate results in a 5.95 percentage point increase in employee participation. Among the other plan characteristics, only the automatic enrollment provision has a significant effect.

The third column shows the effects when additional controls for observable job characteristics, meant to stand in for worker attributes $\overline{X}_{jk}$, are included in the model. These include a dummy for whether the job is unionized, dummies for 9 occupational groups, the average compensation paid workers in the job, and the average compensation squared. With these controls included, the APE of a doubling of the first-dollar match is now a 5.12 percentage point increase. These results are consistent with a small positive

---

[15] These dummies are included in all specifications.
[16] Based on experimentation with various functional forms, specifying the match rate in logs appears to be a reasonable approach. All of the functional forms depicted an effect of match rates on participation that is positive and diminishing. For example, a model in which the first-dollar match is divided into categories of 10-25 percent (excluded), 26-50 percent, 51-75 percent, and >75 percent produced partial effects of 6.20, 12.22, and 11.75, respectively.

sorting effect having been included in the match rate effects shown in the second column. Compensation itself is seen to have a sizable and diminishing effect on participation.

A potential shortcoming of this analysis is that explicit controls for workers' demographic traits have not been included in the measure of $\overline{X}_{jk}$. Many studies of plan participation have included such controls, with varying results. Gender is often found to be insignificant, but some studies show that, among low-earners, men are less likely to participate than women (Papke, 2003; Mitchell, Utkus and Yang, 2005). Education also turns up insignificant in some multivariate analyses, but in other cases (Kusko, Poterba and Wilcox, 1998; Basset, Fleming and Rodrigues, 1998) is found to be positively related to participation. Race is often not included in analyses, but some evidence (Even and MacPherson, 2003; Englehardt and Kumar, 2007) suggests that white workers are more likely to participate than are blacks. The two characteristics that are most consistently found to have positive, significant effects on participation are income and age. As we have seen, the data capture income very well through job-level compensation, and its inclusion in the regression moderates the measure of the effect of employer matches. Whether controlling for age (or any other omitted factor) would also decrease the measure of the match's effect depends on the extent to which workers also sort into high-matching jobs based on these factors.

To explore the effects of demographic traits on 401(k) participation and their potentially biasing impact on the measures of the effects of plan provisions, job averages of various traits were imputed for each observation. These imputations were generated by matching the detailed (3-digit) industry and occupation information, along with the observed wage rate in the job, to 2002 Current Population Statistics data and using regression analysis to predict values for each job. Four demographic variables were produced this way: the average age of workers in the job, the percentage of workers who are male, the percentage having graduated from college, and the percentage who are white.

The fourth and fifth columns of Table 2 give the results of two equations incorporating these variables. In column (4), the broad industry and occupation variables previously included are omitted, while in column (5) these controls are added back in. When the separate occupation and industry controls are excluded, the imputed demographic traits show several effects that are consistent with the literature: age and percent white have significantly positive effects, and percent male is negative but marginally insignificant. Contrary to the literature, the imputed percentage of college graduates has a significantly negative effect on participation. When the broad industry and occupation control are added back in, this education effect becomes positive, and the other measured demographic effects remain in the "right" direction, but they are generally small and statistically insignificant. This suggests that the industry and occupation controls included in column (3) capture some of the same underlying demographics that the imputed demographic variables do. Since the imputed traits improve the log pseudo-likelihood of the model, the full specification in column (5) is preferred. Note that the inclusion of these imputed traits does not reduce the measured effect of the employer match – in fact, the APE of a doubling of the match rises to 5.34 percentage points in column (5).

These first 5 columns of Table 2 have largely applied the cross-sectional approaches that have been applied elsewhere. But, as discussed above, the criticism of those other studies also remains: if the controls entered for $\overline{X}_{jk}$ and E_k are incomplete, leaving substantial unmeasured components $\overline{a}_{jk}$ and c_k, then the measured effects of M_k on P_{jk} may not reflect the pure treatment effect. In particular, we might be most concerned about the effects of worker sorting: even controlling for many worker attributes through the job-level variables $\overline{X}_{jk}$, the residual preferences of workers for generous retirement benefits may still correlate with high participation rates. One approach to solving this difficulty allowed by the National Compensation Survey data used in this study is to include additional control variables capturing workers' revealed preference for receiving compensation in the form of key benefits. Workers who are not interested in saving for retirement – Ippolito's "spenders" – are likely to prefer a larger portion of their compensation in wages. Those who have a high underlying 401(k) participation propensity – Ippolito's "savers" – are likely to prefer other benefits as well instead of wage. This seems especially likely to be true of health benefits.

In column (6) of Table 2, additional controls accounting for the composition of workers' compensations have been included: the wage component of compensation, the health care component, the component associated with any Defined Benefit plan present for the job, and a dummy indicating whether workers in the job have access to another Defined Contribution plan. The results show that a higher health plan component of compensation is significantly associated with higher participation in one's 401(k). The presence of other Defined Contribution plans is also associated with higher participation. These results suggest some savings propensity-related job sorting on these two benefit categories. But similar sorting is not apparent on the wage-nonwage frontier, nor on defined benefit plans. And adding these controls does not reduce our estimate of the effect of the employer match – in fact, it increases it. The APE of doubling the match rate is now 5.90 percentage points. In the rest of the paper, this full-specification cross-sectional model reported in column (6) is referred to as the base model.

In the base model, several of the measured effects of other 401(k) plan provisions are worth noting. First, the APE of automatic enrollment provisions remains at a substantial level: automatic enrollment is seen to increase participation by 7.4 percentage points. This is within the margin of error of the 11 point increase that Madrian and Shea (2001) find studying one large employer. Second, providing workers with a choice of how to invest their own contributions appears to have a small but significant, negative association on participation. This is consistent with the results of Iyengar, Jiang and Huberman (2003) and Choi, Laibson and Madrian (2006), who argue that too much choice can impart complexity costs that reduce plan enrollment. But having choice over the employer's contributions does not appear to have any appreciable effect on participation. Both of these APEs contradict Papke (2003), who finds dramatic positive effects. Finally, the ability to draw loans from one's account has an insignificant effect on participation as well.

Distinguishing dimensions of the match

Another approach to isolating the treatment effect of employer matches on participation is to control for the overall generosity of the plan, as illustrated in equation (3.2) above. Table 3 presents the results obtained by adding our total percentage match variable to the right hand side of the equations analyzed in Table 2^{17}. In every column, the inclusion of the overall generosity measure has reduced the APE of the first dollar match. But this reduction (and the direct effect of the total percentage match) declines and becomes insignificant as more controls are added to the equation. In column (6), we are left with an APE for the first dollar match of .0451. This suggests that the effects observed in the base model may not be distorted much by worker sorting of the type described in our model.

But note that this identification approach relies on two restrictions: the operation of the treatment effect solely through the first-dollar match, and the operation of the sorting effect solely through the total percentage match. Either of these restrictions could be challenged. For instance, the overall generosity of the match may itself have a direct effect on participation; in this case, controlling for the total potential match nets out some of the treatment effect. Alternatively, high first-dollar match rates for a given level of generosity may evidence attempts by employers to coax participation out of workers with below-average savings propensities; in this case, some (negative) sorting on the first-dollar match is not controlled for by the total potential match variable. Thus, while the results of Table 3 are suggestive of some positive sorting on match rates, alternative methods for isolating the treatment effect are desired.

Instrumental Variables Estimation

We can also estimate the treatment effect of the first-dollar match rate on plan participation by instrumenting for the match rate. The model suggests two candidates for valid instruments – the variables that appear in the match determination equation (2.4) but not in the participation equation (1.3). First, the characteristics of an individual's

---

[17] An alternative analysis with total percentage match entered in logs produced very similar results.

coworkers, $\overline{X}_{\sim jk}$, play an integral role in the determination of the match, but they may not affect the individual's participation directly. To exploit this, several measures of $\overline{X}_{\sim jk}$ were calculated from the data. For each job j in establishment k, the average compensation among jobs sampled from k, excluding job j, was measured. In addition, similar calculations were made using each of the imputed demographic characteristics (age, proportion with a college degree, proportion male, and proportion white). Note that these measures embody an additional measurement error. While the object of interest is a measure of the average characteristics of *all* other workers at establishment k, our measure includes only those that were sampled in the National Compensation Survey. But since jobs in each establishment were randomly sampled with probability proportional to the numbers of workers in the jobs, our measure of $\overline{X}_{\sim jk}$ is unbiased.

Two variables were generated to capture O_k. These variables measure the average proportion of compensation paid to defined contribution plans among other employers in the corresponding labor market. They were calculated using the larger NCS dataset measuring employer costs for all units in the NCS panel (not just those that were newly initiated in 2002 or 2003). The first of these measures uses geography to define the relevant labor market, taking advantage of the cluster sample design of the NCS, in which a small set of (predominantly metropolitan) areas is selected as primary sampling units. Within each of these areas, the average fraction of compensation spent by employers on Defined Contribution plans was calculated. The second measure of O_k is calculated similarly, but using 2-digit industry definitions as the relevant labor market concept.

These measures relate somewhat to the instruments used by Even and MacPherson (2005), who instrument for M_k with the demographic characteristics of workers in the same industry-size cells as those in their dataset. Even and MacPherson's results suggest that cross-sectional measures may *under*-estimate the effects of match rates due to *negative* sorting in of workers between jobs. While our instruments are similar in spirit to those of Even and MacPherson, they should better capture significant amounts of variation in M_k. The co-worker measures ($\overline{X}_{\sim jk}$) are similarly based on demographics, but they more directly measure spillovers between workers' demands because they are calculated within employers. The labor market measures (O_k) are similarly based on sectors, but they more directly measure the effects of competition because they are based on measures of DC plan generosity actually dispensed in the relevant markets.

Table 4 presents results obtained by using the instrumental variables methodology described Wooldridge (2005). That is, equation (2.4) describing the determination of M_k was estimated using OLS, and the residuals, $\hat{\eta}_e$, were added to the BQMLE model of participation with the full complement of explanatory variables examined in column (6) of Table 2. The corrected standard errors were then estimated using the methodology described in Papke and Wooldridge (2007). This methodology also readily allows testing of the validity of the instrumental approach: standard t-tests (using the corrected standard errors) can be applied to the estimated coefficient on $\hat{\eta}_e$.

In the top panel of Table 4, the APEs on participation using the instrumental variables methodology are listed. The top row contains the APEs of the first-dollar match rate, and the second row contains the APEs of the first-stage residuals, which includes any endogenous variation relating to worker sorting across plans. The three columns contain the results for different sets of instruments: the co-worker instruments $\overline{X}_{\sim jk}$, the labor market instruments O_k, and the combination of all instruments. These estimates were generated using a slightly reduced sample of 2,372 observations in 464 establishments, as we limit our scrutiny to only those observations for which a full set of instruments could be generated (e.g., establishments having data for only one collected job are excluded).

Instrumenting with the co-worker measures alone, the estimated APE of the first-dollar match rate indicates that a doubling of the match rate increases participation by 17.36 percentage points. This implies that the cross-sectional results shown in Table 2 are influenced by substantial amounts of negative sorting, which is borne out by the substantial (-.1233) and statistically significant estimated APE of the first-stage residual. Using only the labor market instruments, we estimate that the match rate has an even greater effect; the estimated APE is .4532, and both it and the APE of the residual term are statistically significant despite large standard errors. Using all co-worker and labor market instruments, the estimated APE of the log first-dollar match rate is .2147, and the APE of the first-stage residual is again a significantly negative.

These results reinforce those of Even and MacPherson in portraying the determination of match rates as significantly motivated by a desire to increase the saving rates of the workers who have low underlying savings propensities. Such a behavior could be caused by employers having paternalist motives or by their efforts to satisfy the non-discrimination rules that apply to 401(k) plans. If, in fact, this behavior is driven by non-discrimination rules, we might observe differences in how it applies to different populations; we will return to this topic below. Little direct evidence of this dynamic has been documented, but Bernheim and Garrett (2003) and Bayer, Bernheim and Scholz (1996) provide evidence that a similar, "remedial" impetus is prevalent for employer-provided financial education programs.

Confidence in these results depends on the validity of the instruments. The bottom panel of Table 4 provides information from the first stage of each estimation. First, the coefficients from the OLS regressions of the log of the first-dollar match on the instruments is listed (coefficients of all other exogenous variables are suppressed). These coefficients seem generally to be plausible; e.g., having well-paid and well-educated co-workers seems to increase one's match rate. Having older co-workers seems to decrease one's match rate, which contradicts the positive correlation between age and plan participation. But it seems plausible that employers with older workers would have less of an imperative to sort between savers and spenders. The labor market measures both have positive coefficients, although the regional variable is not statistically significant. At the bottom of the table, the partial R-Squared and F-Test on the excluded instruments as discussed by Bound, Jaeger and Baker (1995) and Shea (1997) are listed. These indicate that the instruments are relatively weak, together explaining less than 2 percent of the residual variation in the match rate, but that they are strong enough to assuage concerns about finite-sample bias. The weakness is especially pronounced when the labor market measures are the only instruments; in subsequent tables, we focus on specifications that include co-worker instruments.

The low first-stage R-Squareds in Table 4 make it especially imperative to verify the exogeneity of the instruments. In particular, the exogeneity of $\overline{X}_{\sim jk}$ might be compromised if co-workers directly affect each others' plan participation. As discussed by Duflo and Saez (2002), such network effects can operate through a variety of mechanisms if co-workers have frequent contact with each other. If they do, then our IV estimates of match effects will be biased upward. Duflo and Saez offer some ways of exploring whether network effects are prevalent in our measures of $\overline{X}_{\sim jk}$. They note that university workers in small departments are much more likely to interact with each other directly than those in large departments; therefore, the network effects will be more pronounced in small departments. In fact, their analysis shows no significant network effects within larger departments.

We can apply this insight to our analysis, with a complication: a maximum of 8 jobs are sampled within each NCS respondent, so $\overline{X}_{\sim jk}$ is measured with greater error among large establishments in our data. So while direct networking effects in large establishments may be limited, the measure of co-worker demand for matches is also less reliable. An intermediate group of establishments have the highest potential for well-measured demand effects that are not affected by direct networking effects: establishments with between 100 and 500 employers are sampled with the full 8 jobs (smaller establishments yield lower numbers of jobs) but are big enough to significantly dampen any network effects.

Table 5 depicts the results of our analysis as applied to large, mid-sized, and small establishments. The first column lists the sample sizes of each group; while the observation counts vary widely, the groups have relatively similar establishment counts. In the second column, we list the APEs from the base model as applied to the restricted sample. These results show a higher match effect among mid-sized establishments, where the APE is .1394. The APEs among large and small establishments are statistically insignificant. When we apply our instrumental variables to these samples in column (3), we see possible evidence of endogeneity in the co-worker instruments. We estimate significantly higher APEs, and significant negative sorting, among the small establishments, where networks effects are most likely. But no significant sorting is measured among mid-sized establishments, where we expect networking effects, if any, to be small. These results are consistent with endogeneity problems in the instruments. On the other hand, the results also show negative sorting (and higher APEs) among the largest employers, where networking effects are least likely, and these effects are statistically significant despite larger standard errors.

Duflo and Saez offer an alternative approach to dealing with this potential endogeneity. In their study, when the co-worker measures match dissimilar workers, networking effects become insignificant. In column (4), this insight is applied: we use adjusted co-worker measures that are calculated only using co-workers who do not share the same (1-digit) occupation as the reference worker. Using these adjusted instruments, we obtain a smaller APE for the full sample, but the APE is still notably higher than the base model measure. The APEs measured within establishment sizes diminish significantly, with the APE among small establishments now statistically insignificant. Most strikingly, the APEs among mid-size and large establishments are .2170 and .2112, respectively; both are statistically significant. These results indicate that match rates have substantial effects on plan participation and suggest that the base model may underestimate these effects. But while the adjusted instruments instill greater confidence about their exogeneity, they are even weaker in the first stage, causing the associated standard errors to be high. Consequently, the coefficients on $\hat{\eta}_e$ are not statistically significant. Nonetheless, the evidence indicates that the base results are not upwardly biased and are likely to be downwardly biased by negative sorting in the matching of workers and match rates.

Differences by Income Level

In Table 6, the APEs are measured separately for three income groups. Columns (2) and (3) report the APEs for the log first dollar match and the automatic enrollment provision, respectively, estimated from the base, cross-sectional equation. These results indicate large differences in behavior between the income groups. The match rate has small but significant measured effects among the high- and middle-income groups, but no effect on the low-income group. The automatic enrollment provision, however, is negligible among the high-income group and very large – with an APE of .2367 – among the low-income group; the middle-income group displays an intermediate automatic enrollment effect.

In columns (4) and (5), instrumental variables estimates for the income groups are shown, with both co-worker and labor market instruments employed, and separate columns for the two alternative sets of co-worker measures. In the high-income group, the APEs of the match rate fall considerably and are significantly negative, and the (positive) sorting effect is also significant. Among the middle-income group, the APEs rise considerably and negative sorting is evident, although the sorting is again not statistically significant. Among the low income group, the APEs continue to be negligible, and sorting is not evident.

These results portray a compelling story about 401(k) participation that was obscured when we studied the entire sample together. The positive sorting among high earners suggests that these workers may have a high amount of bargaining power with their employers – high earners wishing to save in a 401(k) may effectively push for higher matches. Alternatively, employers' desire to sort between "savers" and "spenders" may be especially great among high earners. But once these workers have been sorted, they are not attracted to greater participation by higher match rates. Consistent with this story, these workers are also unresponsive to automatic enrollment provisions.

Middle income workers, however, seem to be quite responsive to the match rate in deciding whether to participate in their 401(k) plans. The APEs in Table 6 indicate that a doubling of the match rate will add more than 20 percentage points to their participation rates. These workers, with relatively high levels of income despite qualifying as non-highly compensated workers (NHCEs), and behaviorally responsive to the match rate, are prime targets for employers needing to (remedially) boost NHCE contributions to meet non-discrimination rules. The apparent negative sorting on match rates seen in this group is consistent with this characterization. Perhaps most interestingly middle-income workers may be more responsive to significant match rate increases than they are to the implementation of automatic enrollment provisions. Therefore, matching contributions may have a significant role to play in encouraging saving among the middle class. This is a significant departure from the growing literature discussed earlier.

Among low earners, the story told by the emerging literature re-appears. Low income workers do not appear to be influenced at all by matching provisions, either in the participation decision or in sorting themselves among workers. At the same time these workers are greatly influenced by automatic enrollment. This suggests passive decision-making about saving and a low amount of bargaining power with employers.

Conclusion

In this study, I have re-examined and added to a large and growing body of evidence on the determinants of participation in 401(k) plans, paying particularly close attention to the effects of employer matches. This focus is timely, since matching provisions have been fading from the attention of many who have offered automatic enrollment as a better solution to the problem of under-saving. The previous literature on this topic has covered a wide range of methods, each with its own pros and cons. It has exploited a wide range of datasets, most of which lack generalizability. And it has made few comparisons between the effects of the match and the effects of automatic enrollment. Consequently, it has produced a wide range of estimates that are hard to synthesize and even harder to put into perspective.

By employing several estimation strategies, placing them within a single framework, and using a large, broad dataset that has information on many aspects of 401(k) plan provisions, this study is able to offer some clarity to the issue. Considering the population as a whole, I find that the level of the employer match has a significant effect on plan participation, and that this effect is observed not because workers positively sort into generous plans, but because they respond rationally to the marginal incentives when deciding whether to participate. This may be welcome news to those who have wondered at the lack of rationality identified in the recent literature on automatic enrollment.

The most illuminating results come when workers of different income groups are considered separately. The results among lower-income workers reinforce the recent literature, with automatic enrollment producing large effects and matching contributions none. This implies that the recent efforts to encourage automatic enrollment provisions have been appropriate ways to increase retirement saving among this group. But among intermediate-level earners, the picture is less clear. This group shows significant responses to employer matches that may be larger than those associated with automatic enrollment. Thus policies to encourage and/or maintain retirement savings among the middle class should advocate a significant role for traditional incentives of this nature. Finally, the results provide a picture of the underlying determination of the matches themselves: higher matches appear to be aimed at sorting and attracting workers among the highest level of earnings, and/or to stimulating savings among middle-earning workers. This implies that the non-discrimination rules governing 401(k) plans are an important consideration of employers setting up retirement plans.

References

Bassett, William, Michael Fleming and Anthony Rodrigues. (1998) "How Workers use 401(k) Plans: The Participation, Contribution, and Withdrawal Decisions." *National Tax Journal*, Vol. 51, No. 2, pp. 263-288.

Bayer, Patrick J., B. Douglas Bernheim and John Karl Scholz, (1996) "The Effects of Financial Education in the Workplace: Evidence from a Survey of Employers," NBER Working Paper 5655.

Bernheim, B. Douglas and Daniel M. Garrett. (2003) "The Effects of Financial Education in the Workplace: Evidence from a Survey of Households." *Journal of Public Economics*, Vol. 87, Issues 7-8, pp. 1487-1519.

Beshears, John, James J. Choi, David Laibson and Brigitte C. Madrian. (2007) "The Impact of Employer Matching on Savings Plan Participation Under Automatic Enrollment." NBER Working Paper 13352.

Brady, Peter J. (2007). "Pension Nondiscrimination Rules and the Incentive to Cross Subsidize Employees." *Journal of Pension Economics and Finance*, Vol. 6, pp 127-145.

Bound, John, David A. Jaeger and Regina Baker. (1995) "Problems with Instrumental Variables Estimation When the Correlation between the Instruments and the Endogenous Explanatory Variable Is Weak." *Journal of the American Statistical Association*, Vol. 90, pp. 443-450.

Choi, James J., Laibson, David I. and Madrian, Brigitte C. (2004) "Plan Design and 401(k) Savings Outcomes." NBER Working Paper W10486.

_____. (2006) "Reducing the Complexity Costs of 401(k) Participation Through Quick Enrollment." NBER Working Paper No. W11979.

Choi, James, David Laibson, Brigitte Madrian and Andrew Metrick. (2002) "Defined Contributions Pensions: Plan Rules, Participant Decisions, and the Path of Least Resistance." In James M. Poterba, ed. *Tax policy and the economy.* Vol. 16. Cambridge, MA: MIT Press, pp. 67-113.

Clark, Robert L. and Schieber, Sylvester. (1998) "Factors Affecting Participation Rates and Contribution Levels in 401(k) Plans." In Olivia S, Mitchell and Sylvester Scheiber ed., *Living With Defined Contribution Pensions: Remaking Responsibility for Retirement.* Philadelphia: University of Pennsylvania Press, pp. 69-96.

Cunningham, Christopher and Gary Engelhardt. (2002) "Federal Tax Policy, Employer Matching, and 401(k) Saving: Evidence from HRS W-2 Records." *National Tax Journal*. Vol. 55, No. 3, pp. 617-645.

Duflo, Esther and Emmanuel Saez. (2002) "Participation and Investment Decisions in a Retirement Plan: the Influence of Colleagues' Choices" *Journal of Public Economics*, vol. 85(1), pages 121-148.

Dworak-Fisher, Keenan. (2007) "Employer generosity in employer-matched 401(k) plans, 2002–03." *Monthly Labor Review*. September 2007, Vol. 130, No. 9.

Employee Benefit Retirement Institute (2002) "The 2002 Small Employer Retirement Survey (SERS) Summary of Findings." http://www.ebri.org/pdf/surveys/sers/2002/02sersof.pdf.

Engelhardt, Gary and Anil Kumar. (2007) "Employer matching and 401(k) saving: Evidence from the health and retirement study" *Journal of Public Economics*. Vol. 91, Issue 10, pp.1920-1943.

Even, William E., and David A. Macpherson. (2005) "The Effects of Employer Matching in 401(k) Plans." *Industrial Relations: A Journal of Economy and Society*. Vol. 44 Issue 3, pp. 525 – 549.

Holmer, Martin; Asa Janney and Bob Cohen. (2008) "Pensim Overview." *Mimeo*, U.S. Department of Labor, July 2008. http://www.polsim.com/overview.pdf.

Ippolito, Richard A. (2002) "Stayers as "Workers" and "Savers": Toward Reconciling the Pension-Quit Literature." *The Journal of Human Resources*, Vol. 37, No. 2. pp. 275-308.

Iyengar, Sheena S., Wei Jiang, and Gur Huberman, 2004. "How Much Choice Is Too Much?: Contributions to 401(k) Retirement Plans," In Olivia Mitchell and Stephen Utkus, eds., *Pension Design and Structure: New Lessons from Behavioral Finance* (Oxford, UK: Oxford University Press): pp. 83-96.

Kusko, Andrea; Poterba, James and Wilcox, David. "Employee Decisions With Respect to 401(k) Plans." (1998) In Olivia S, Mitchell and Sylvester Scheiber ed., *Living With Defined Contribution Pensions: Remaking Responsibility for Retirement*. Philadelphia: University of Pennsylvania Press, pp. 69-96.

Madrian, Brigitte and Shea, Dennis. (2001) "The Power of Suggestion: Inertia in 401(k) Participation and Savings Behavior." *Quarterly Journal of Economics*. Vol. 116, No. 4, pp. 1149-1187.

Mitchell, Olivia S., Stephen P. Utkus and Tongxuan Yang. (2005) "Turning Workers into Savers? Incentives, Liquidity, and Choice in 401(k) Plan Design" NBER Working Paper No. W11726.

Munnell, Alicia H., Annika Sunden and Catherine Taylor. (2001/2) "What Determines 401(k) Participation and Contributions?" *Social Security Bulletin*, Vol. 64, No. 3, pp. 64-75.

Papke, Leslie. (1995) "Participation in and Contributions to 401(k) Pension Plans: Evidence from Plan Data." *Journal of Human Resources*, Vol. 30, No. 2, pp. 311-325.

_____. (2003) "Individual financial decisions in retirement saving plans: the role of participant-direction." *Journal of Public Economics*, Vol. 88, pp. 39-61.

Papke, Leslie and Wooldridge, Jeffrey M. (1996) "Econometric Methods for Fractional Response Variables With an Application to 401(k) Plan Participation Rates." *Journal of Applied Econometrics*, Vol. 11, pp. 619-632.

_____. (2007) "Panel Data Methods for Fractional Response Variables with an Application to Test Pass Rates." *Mimeo*, Michigan State University.

Powell, Robert. "Addition by Subtraction: Eliminating 401(k) matches might actually be a savings boon," *Marketwatch.com*, July 16, 2008.

Shea, John. (1997) "Instrument Relevance in Multivariate Linear Models: A Simple Measure." *Review of Economics and Statistics*, 79:2, pp. 348-352.

U.S. Bureau of Labor Statistics Summary 05-01.

Wooldridge, Jeffrey M. (2002), *Econometric Analysis of Cross Section and Panel Data*. MIT Press: Cambridge, MA.

_____. (2005), "Unobserved Heterogeneity and Estimation of Average Partial Effects," in *Identification and Inference for Econometric Models: Essays in Honor of Thomas Rothenberg*. D.W.K. Andrews and J.H. Stock (eds.). Cambridge: Cambridge University Press, 27-55.

Figure 1: Match and Participation Frequencies in NCS Sample

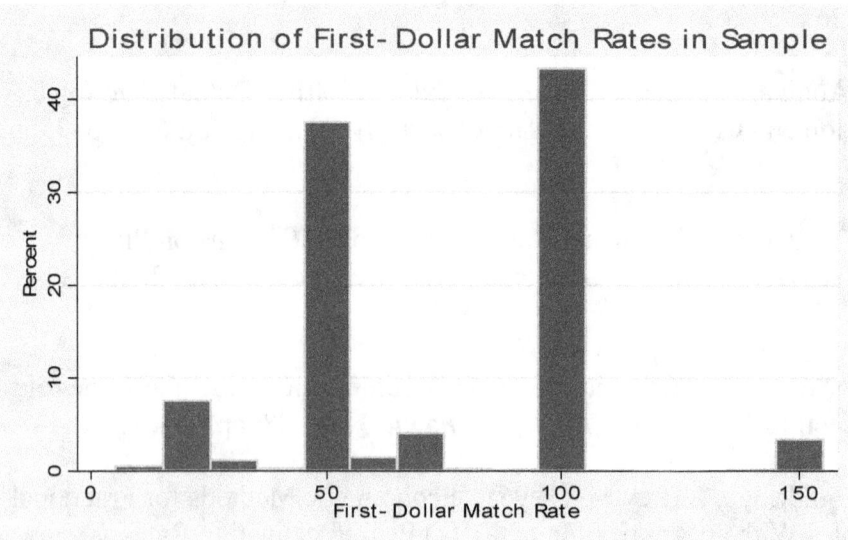

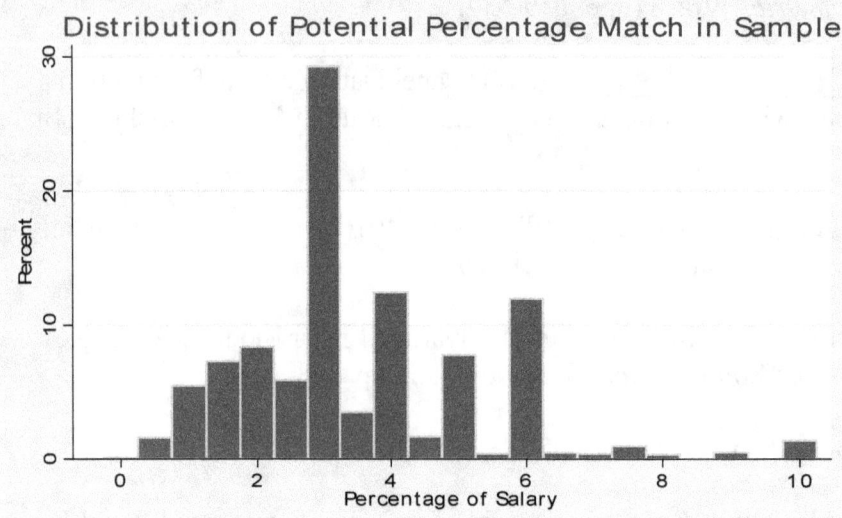

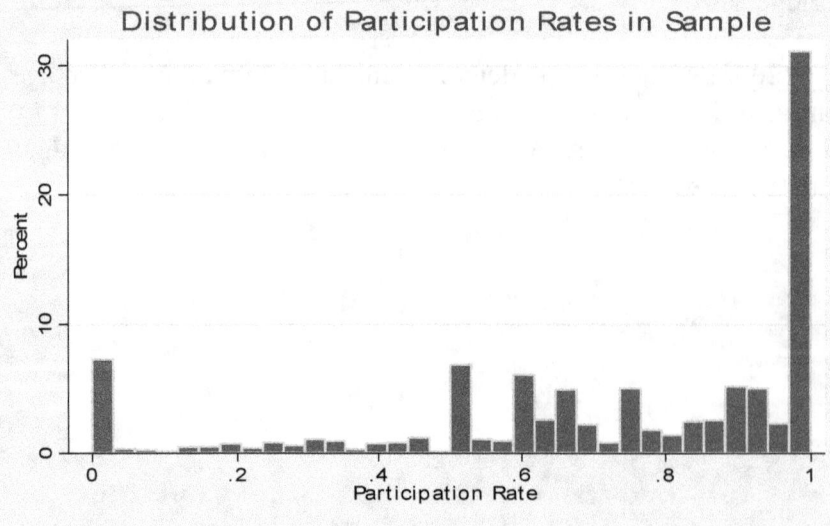

Table 1: Summary Statistics for NCS Data Sample
(2,708 jobs in 587 establishments)

Variable	Mean	Standard Deviation
Participation Rate	0.72	0.30
Match Provisions		
Type of match		
Flat	0.82	0.38
Varies by Contribution	0.13	0.34
Varies by Tenure	0.04	0.21
Generosity		
First Dollar Match Rate	75.37	37.27
Last Dollar Match Rate	68.64	32.36
Percent of Salary Matched	5.16	1.96
Potential Percentage Match	3.57	1.98
Potential Dollar Match	1,657	1,644
Other Plan Provisions		
Control of EE Contribs	0.85	0.36
Control of ER Contribs	0.75	0.43
Availability of Loans	0.70	0.46
Automatic Enrollment	0.06	0.23
Compensation		
Total Compensation	33.10	23.35
Wage	22.62	16.21
Health Cost	2.20	1.19
DB Cost	0.52	1.40
DB Coverage	0.40	0.49
Other DC	0.21	0.41
Data Details		
Year= 2003	0.67	0.47
Establishment Characteristics		
Size: Less than 20	0.09	0.29
Size: 20-50	0.06	0.24
Size: 50-100	0.10	0.30
Size: 100-250	0.16	0.36
Size: 250-500	0.14	0.35
Size: 500-1,000	0.12	0.33
Size: 1,000-2,500	0.13	0.34
Size: 2,500-5,000	0.11	0.31
Size: 5000-10,000	0.06	0.23
Size: Greater than 10,000	0.03	0.16
New England	0.06	0.23
Middle Atlantic	0.15	0.36
East North Central	0.17	0.37
West North Central	0.09	0.28
South Atlantic	0.16	0.37
East South Central	0.02	0.14
West South Central	0.16	0.37
Mountain	0.10	0.30
Pacific	0.10	0.30
Mining/Construction	0.05	0.22
Manufacturing	0.18	0.38
Transportation/Utilities	0.07	0.26
Trade	0.18	0.38
FIRE	0.25	0.44
Services	0.06	0.24
Public Administration	0.21	0.41
Job Characteristics		
Unionization	0.05	0.22

Table 2: Estimated Average Partial Effects on 401(k) Participation with First-Dollar Match as Sole Generosity Measure
(robust standard errors in parentheses)

	Base	Employer Characteristics Included	Job Characteristics Included	Imputed Demographics		Compensation Components Included
	(1)	(2)	(3)	(4)	(5)	(6)
Log of First-Dollar Match	0.0590 (0.0202)	0.0595 (0.0203)	0.0512 (0.0185)	0.0550 (0.0187)	0.0534 (0.0185)	0.0590 (0.0191)
Other Plan Provisions						
Automatic Enrollment		0.0862 (0.0387)	0.0871 (0.0376)	0.0886 (0.0400)	0.0834 (0.0380)	0.0741 (0.0419)
Investment Choice (Own Contribs)		-0.0471 (0.0344)	-0.0563 (0.0320)	-0.0706 (0.0325)	-0.0541 (0.0318)	-0.0571 (0.0317)
Investment Choice (Employer Contribs)		0.0160 (0.0311)	0.0201 (0.0291)	0.0319 (0.0300)	0.0287 (0.0280)	0.0156 (0.0291)
Loan Availability		-0.0057 (0.0233)	-0.0165 (0.0210)	-0.0117 (0.0215)	-0.0171 (0.0210)	-0.0186 (0.0208)
Job-Level Attributes						
Compensation			0.0079 (0.0008)	0.0080 (0.0012)	0.0069 (0.0012)	0.0073 (0.0018)
Compensation Squared			-0.000029 (0.000004)	-0.000030 (0.000005)	-0.000026 (0.000005)	-0.000020 (0.000005)
Imputed Demographics						
Average Age				0.0045 (0.0023)	0.0023 (0.0024)	0.0037 (0.0024)
Percent College Grad				-0.0747 (0.0408)	0.0730 (0.0703)	0.0721 (0.0707)
Percent White				0.4001 (0.1270)	0.1468 (0.1469)	0.1528 (0.1456)
Percent Male				-0.0428 (0.0262)	-0.0193 (0.0323)	-0.0075 (0.0323)
Compensation Components						
Wage						-0.0032 (0.0020)
Defined Benefit Cost						-0.0030 (0.0080)
Health Cost						0.0320 (0.0091)
Other DC Plan Present						0.0826 (0.0230)
Other Controls						
Region and Estab Size Controls	No	Yes	Yes	Yes	Yes	Yes
Industry Controls	No	Yes	Yes	Yes	Yes	Yes
Union, Occupation Controls	No	No	Yes	No	Yes	Yes

Table 3: Estimated Average Partial Effects on 401(k) Participation with First-Dollar Match and Total Percentage Match Separated
(robust standard errors in parentheses)

	Base	Employer Characteristics Included	Job Characteristics Included	Imputed Demographics Included		Compensation Components Included
	(1)	(2)	(3)	(4)	(5)	(6)
Log of First-Dollar Match	0.0254	0.0350	0.0371	0.0338	0.0384	0.0451
	(0.0268)	(0.0251)	(0.0227)	(0.0233)	(0.0229)	(0.0232)
Total Percentage Match	0.0141	0.0105	0.0060	0.0091	0.0065	0.0061
	(0.0077)	(0.0073)	(0.0064)	(0.0068)	(0.0065)	(0.0063)
Other Plan Provisions						
Automatic Enrollment		0.0901	0.0896	0.0917	0.0859	0.0767
		(0.0388)	(0.0379)	(0.0400)	(0.0383)	(0.0422)
Investment Choice (Own Contribs)		-0.0550	-0.0608	-0.0769	-0.0588	-0.0613
		(0.0347)	(0.0324)	(0.0330)	(0.0323)	(0.0321)
Investment Choice (Employer Contribs)		0.0219	0.0234	0.0369	0.0210	0.0187
		(0.0319)	(0.0297)	(0.0310)	(0.0293)	(0.0296)
Loan Availability		-0.0056	-0.0163	-0.0121	-0.0169	-0.0184
		(0.0233)	(0.0210)	(0.0215)	(0.0210)	(0.0208)
Job-Level Attributes						
Compensation			0.0078	0.0078	0.0067	0.0072
			(0.0008)	(0.0012)	(0.0012)	(0.0018)
Compensation Squared			-0.000028	-0.000029	-0.000025	-0.000020
			(0.000004)	(0.000005)	(0.000005)	(0.000005)
Imputed Demographics						
Average Age				0.0048	0.0025	0.0039
				(0.0023)	(0.0024)	(0.0024)
Percent College Grad				-0.0713	0.0737	0.0723
				(0.0408)	(0.0704)	(0.0708)
Percent White				0.3944	0.1475	0.1538
				(0.1273)	(0.1470)	(0.1453)
Percent Male				-0.0409	-0.0191	-0.0075
				(0.0262)	(0.0322)	(0.0321)
Compensation Components						
Wage						-0.0031
						(0.0020)
Defined Benefit Cost						-0.0033
						(0.0080)
Health Cost						0.0320
						(0.0091)
Other DC Plan Present						0.0823
						(0.0230)
Other Controls						
Region and Estab Size Controls	No	Yes	Yes	Yes	Yes	Yes
Industry Controls	No	Yes	Yes	Yes	Yes	Yes
Union, Occupation Controls	No	No	Yes	No	Yes	Yes

Table 4: Details of Instrumental Variables Analysis (Instruments Include All Co-Workers)
(robust standard errors in parentheses)

	Co-Worker Characteristics Only	Market Measures Only	Co-Worker Characteristics And Market Measures
	(1)	(2)	(3)
Average Partial Effects of Match			
Log of First-Dollar Match	0.1736	0.4532	0.2147
	(0.0741)	(0.1819)	(0.0618)
First-Stage Residual	-0.1233	-0.4036	-0.1659
	(0.0747)	(0.1832)	(0.0633)
First-Stage Coefficients			
Co-Workers' Compensation	0.0095		0.0091
	(0.0038)		(0.0037)
Co-Workers' Compensation Squared	-0.000073		-0.000069
	(0.000031)		(0.000031)
Co-Workers' Age	-0.0159		-0.0168
	(0.0054)		(0.0054)
Co-Workers' Percent Male	-0.1758		-0.2171
	(0.0701)		(0.0709)
Co-Workers' Percent White	-0.5891		-0.6270
	(0.2883)		(0.2880)
Co-Workers' Percent College Graduate	0.0680		0.0665
	(0.0947)		(0.0945)
Other Employers' DC Fraction in Area		1.9710	1.8154
		(1.8785)	(1.8770)
Other Employers' DC Fraction in Industry		5.9911	7.1124
		(1.8274)	(1.8725)
First-Stage Diagnostics			
Partial R-Squared	0.0104	0.0050	0.0168
Adjusted F-Test	24.97	11.90	40.70

Table 5: Instrumental Variables Results by Establishment Size
(robust standard errors in parentheses)
Third Line: Significance of Instrument (.10 los)
Fourth Line: First-Stage Partial R-Squared

Sample	Sample Size Observations (Establishments)	Base Results	Instrumental Variables	
			Co-Worker Characteristics And Market Measures	Adjusted Co-Worker Characteristics And Market Measures
	(1)	(2)	(3)	(4)
All Observations	2372 (464)	0.0522 (0.0209)	0.2147 (0.0618) Yes 0.0168	0.1410 (0.0701) No 0.0120
Establishment Employment >500	1120 (171)	0.0319 (0.0324)	0.2298 (0.1051) Yes 0.0430	0.2112 (0.1185) No 0.0307
Establishment Employment 100-500	711 (143)	0.1394 (0.0391)	0.0755 (0.0773) No 0.0932	0.2170 (0.0735) No 0.0826
Establishment Employment <=500	541 (150)	-0.0103 (0.0367)	0.2000 (0.1336) Yes 0.0565	0.1336 (0.1429) No 0.0524

Table 6: Instrumental Variables Results by Compensation Level
(robust standard errors in parentheses)
Third Line: Significance of Instrument (.10 los)
Fourth Line: First-Stage Partial R-Squared

Sample	Sample Size Observations (Establishments) (1)	Base Results (2)	Automatic Enrollment Effect (3)	IV Results	
				Co-Worker Characteristics And Market Measures (4)	Adjusted Co-Worker Characteristics And Market Measures (5)
All Observations	2372 (461)	0.0522 (0.0209)	0.1040 (0.0395)	0.2147 (0.0618) Yes 0.0168	0.1410 (0.0701) No 0.0120
Average Hourly Compensation >=$36	788 (293)	0.0532 (0.0238)	0.0334 (0.0365)	-0.1796 (0.0782) Yes 0.0448	-0.1782 (0.0715) Yes 0.0511
Average Hourly Compensation $21-36	785 (350)	0.0589 (0.0288)	0.1219 (0.0395)	0.2096 (0.1574) No 0.0180	0.2506 (0.1439) No 0.0200
Average Hourly Compensation <$21	805 (150)	-0.0026 (0.0328)	0.2367 (0.0613)	0.0597 (0.1985) No 0.0341	-0.0060 (0.2955) No 0.0159

www.ingramcontent.com/pod-product-compliance
Lightning Source LLC
Chambersburg PA
CBHW081759170526
45167CB00008B/3257